SYMPHONIES DE BEETHOVEN

Partition de Piano

dediée au Baron H. de Bülow

par
F. LISZT.

Vol. I.

Arrangement propriété des éditeurs.

Leipzig, Breitkopf & Härtel.

Pr. 9 Mark netto.

12172. I.

Beethoven Symphonies
Nos. 1–5
Transcribed for Solo Piano

FRANZ LISZT

Introduction by
Alan Walker

DOVER PUBLICATIONS, INC.
Mineola, New York

Bibliographical Note

This Dover edition, first published in 1998, is an unabridged republication of Volume 1 of *Symphonies de Beethoven / Partition de Piano / dediée au Baron H. de Bülow / par F. Liszt,* originally published by Breitkopf & Härtel, Leipzig, [1865].
This Dover edition adds a frontispiece, a glossary, and new main headings throughout. Dr. Alan Walker graciously provided the following materials, drawn or adapted from portions of his three-volume work *Franz Liszt,* originally published by Alfred A. Knopf, New York, in 1983, 1989 and 1996: a facsimile of Liszt's handwritten French preface to his Beethoven transcriptions, together with its English translation; and an introduction adapted from the biography.

International Standard Book Number: 0-486-40114-6

Manufactured in the United States of America
Dover Publications, Inc., 31 East 2nd Street, Mineola, N.Y. 11501

CONTENTS

Liszt's piano transcriptions of Beethoven's nine symphonies were originally published by Breitkopf & Härtel, Leipzig, in 1865. The complete edition was dedicated to conductor and virtuoso pianist Hans von Bülow, Liszt's favorite student, later his son-in-law. The transcription of Symphony No. 5, begun in 1836—the first of the complete set—was originally dedicated to the painter Jean-Auguste-Dominique Ingres. Humphrey Searle catalogued the complete set of transcriptions as S464; Peter Raabe, as R376.

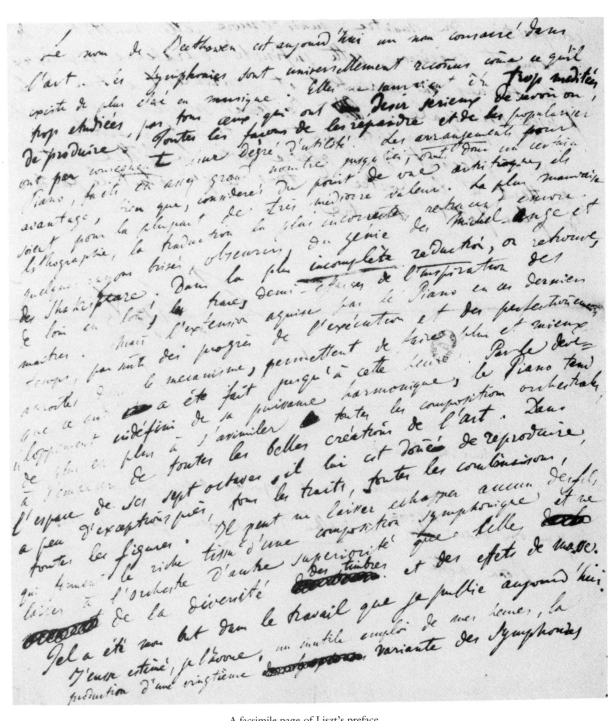

A facsimile page of Liszt's preface
to his piano transcriptions of the Beethoven symphonies

(Courtesy of Alan Walker)

Preface

The name of Beethoven is sacred in art. His symphonies are nowadays universally recognized to be masterpieces. No one who seriously desires to extend his knowledge, or create something new himself, can ever devote sufficient thought to them, or ever study them enough. That is why every way of making them widely known and popular has some merit; not that the rather numerous arrangements published so far are without a certain merit, though for the most part deeper study readily reduces their value. The poorest lithograph, the faultiest translation, always gives an idea, however vague, of the genius of a Michelangelo and of a Shakespeare; and even the most imperfect piano arrangement will now and then reveal traces, a little obliterated perhaps, of a master's inspiration. But the advances the piano has gained of late, in both the technique of performance and in mechanical improvement, make it possible to produce more and better arrangements than ever before. As a result of the vast development of its harmonic power, the piano is trying more and more to take possession of all orchestral compositions. Within the compass of its seven octaves it is capable, with but a few exceptions, of reproducing all the features, all the combinations, and all the configurations of the deepest musical creations. And it leaves to the orchestra no other advantages than those of contrasting tone colors and mass effects—immense advantages, to be sure.

Such has been my aim in the work I lay before the public today. I confess that I should have to regard it as a rather useless employment of my time if I had produced just another version of the Symphonies in a manner up to now routine. But I shall think my time well spent if I have succeeded in transferring to the piano not only the grand outlines of Beethoven's compositions but also those multitude of details and finer points that make such a significant contribution to the perfection of the whole. I will be satisfied if I stand on the level of the intelligent engraver, or the conscientious translator, who grasps the spirit of a work and thus contributes to our insight into the great masters and to our sense of the beautiful.

Franz Liszt
Rome, 1865
Translated from the original French by Alan Walker

Liszt and the Beethoven Symphonies

Between June 1863 and April 1865, while in devotional studies in his small cell at the Oratory of the Madonna del Rosario, outside Rome, Liszt brought to completion his remarkable series of piano transcriptions of the Beethoven symphonies. Perhaps the most piquant part of the business was that much of the creative work was done on an antiquated *pianino* (with a missing D!), and the first ears to hear the strains of these arrangements were those of the Domenican brothers. On April 25, Liszt received the tonsure at the Vatican—a major turning-point in his life—and entered Holy Orders. He even lived in the Vatican for a time, and that is where he checked the proofs of these transcriptions.

The task of transcription had occupied Liszt, off and on, for nearly thirty years. In 1836—in his heyday as a young virtuoso, and single-mindedly devoted to the memory of Beethoven—Liszt had begun work on the Fifth Symphony, possibly with little thought that he might one day tackle the entire set. But by 1839 he had completed the Fifth, Sixth and Seventh Symphonies, as well as the Funeral March from the "Eroica," premiering his transcription of the "Pastorale" in Vienna with such success that it would become something of a recital warhorse with him.

The impulse to complete the entire set came from the publishers Breitkopf and Härtel. Aware of what Liszt had already accomplished, they urged him to tackle the other works. Liszt agreed, on condition that he be allowed to revise his earlier efforts and issue all nine symphonies together. To help him get started, Breitkopf sent Liszt the orchestral scores in their own "critically revised" editions.

Nobody understood the art of transcription better than Liszt, yet even he regarded these symphonies as a difficult prospect for one pair of hands. In his preface to the collection [*see p. vii*] he declared his aims:

> . . . I shall think my time well spent if I have succeeded in transferring to the piano not only the grand outlines of Beethoven's compositions but also those multitude of details and finer points that make such a significant contribution to the perfection of the whole.

What gripped his imagination was the challenge these symphonies represented in defying ten fingers to reproduce them *without harming Beethoven's thought*. The results were spectacular, a model of their kind: the transcriptions remain unsurpassed in the amount of fine orchestral detail incorporated into their texture, and their solutions—often of seemingly impossible technical problems—are carried out in the most pianistic way. One need only compare Liszt's solutions to those that preceded him: Kalkbrenner's (in 1840), Hummel's (before 1837) and, above all, Czerny's (1827–9). As a function of his art, Liszt understood that a liberty judiciously taken could bring the "truth" of a passage more directly to the listener: "In matters of translation," he once remarked, "there are some exactitudes that are the equivalent of infidelities."

There is a revealing postscript to Liszt's Beethoven symphony transcriptions. Two years after they were published, Breitkopf and Härtel invited Liszt to tackle the string quartets—ostensibly a far simpler task.

In October 1866 he wrote to the firm, after having wrestled with the pieces for several months:

> It is very mortifying to me to have to confess that I have most awkwardly come to a standstill with the transcription of the Beethoven Quartets. After several attempts the result was either absolutely *unplayable*—or insipid stuff. Nevertheless, I shall not give up my project, and shall make another trial to solve this problem of pianoforte arrangement. If I succeed I will at once inform you of my "Eureka."

He never did succeed. The reason, as his letter makes clear, was his unwillingness to publish anything unplayable. As for the playable, that was merely pointless to him where the result was simply to obscure Beethoven's intentions. Time and again, these are the principles on which Liszt refuses to yield. They raise his transcriptions above the humdrum level of the mere "piano reduction" to that of great art.

Alan Walker

Dr. Alan Walker is author of *Franz Liszt*, a work in three volumes: *The Virtuoso Years, 1811–1847; The Weimar Years, 1848–1861;* and *The Final Years, 1861–1886.* The volumes were published by Alfred Knopf, New York, in 1983, 1989 and 1996, respectively; and by Cornell University Press, New York, in 1987, 1993 and 1997. Dr. Walker is also author of *Schumann: The Man and the Musician* (Barrie & Jenkins Ltd., London, 1972) and editor of *The Chopin Companion* (W. W. Norton, New York, 1973). He is on the faculty of The School of Art, Drama & Music, McMaster University, Hamilton, Ontario, Canada.

GLOSSARY

Orchestral instrument names and other terms in the piano score

Alto(s) = violas

Basses – contrabasses (string basses) [also see *C.B.*]
Basson(s) = bassoon(s)

Celli(s) [also see *Violonc.*]
C. B. [*Contrebasses*] = contrabasses (string basses)
Clar(inette) = clarinet
Cors = French horns

et = and

Flute(s), Fl.

Hautb(ois) = oboe

Instr(uments) à cordes, I. à c. = stringed instruments
Instr(uments) à vent, I. à v. = wind instruments

Péd(ale) à chaque mesure = separate pedal for each measure
pizz(icato) = plucked
pour le Piano à 7 octaves = for a 7-octave piano [*see p. 190*]

seul(s) = alone

Timb(ales) = timpani (kettle drums)
    (appears once as *Timballes*)
Tous l'orchestre, Tutti = full orchestra
Trombones
Tromp(ettes) = trumpets

Viola [also see *Alto*]
Viol., Violons = violins
    (appears once as the German *Violinen*)
Violonc(elles) = cellos

Symphony No. 1
in C Major, Op. 21

1

Symphony No. 2

in D Major, Op. 36

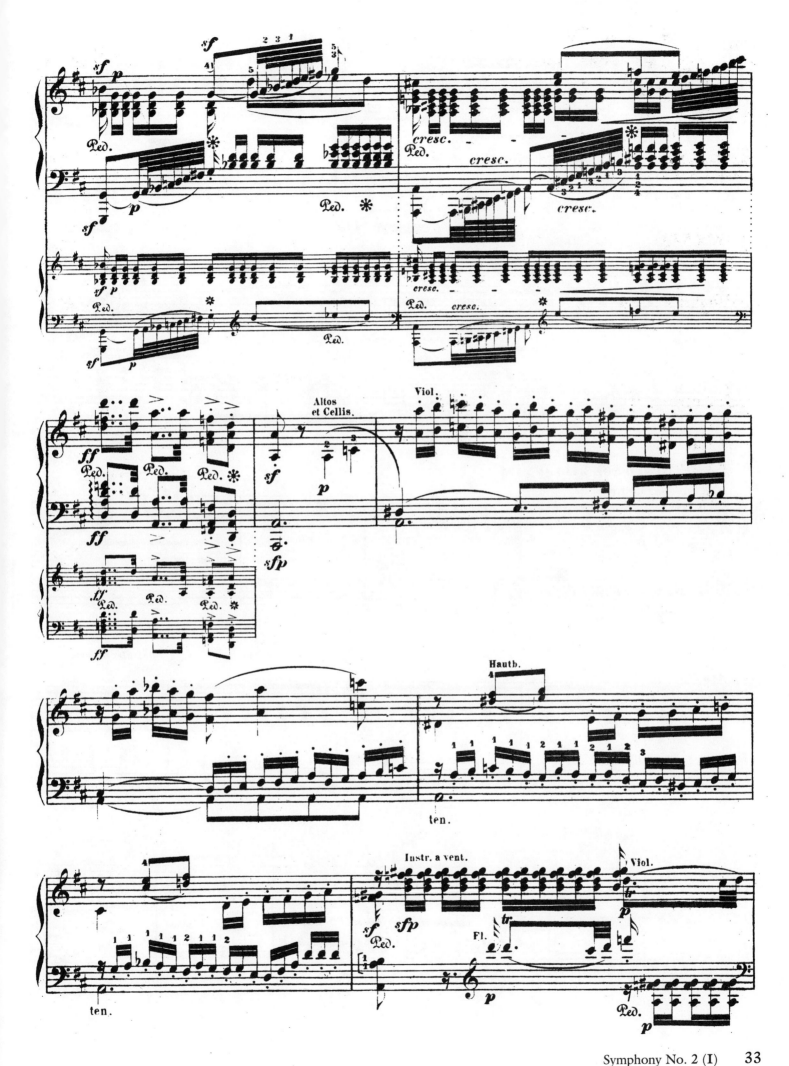

Allegro con brio. ($\sharp$ = 100.)

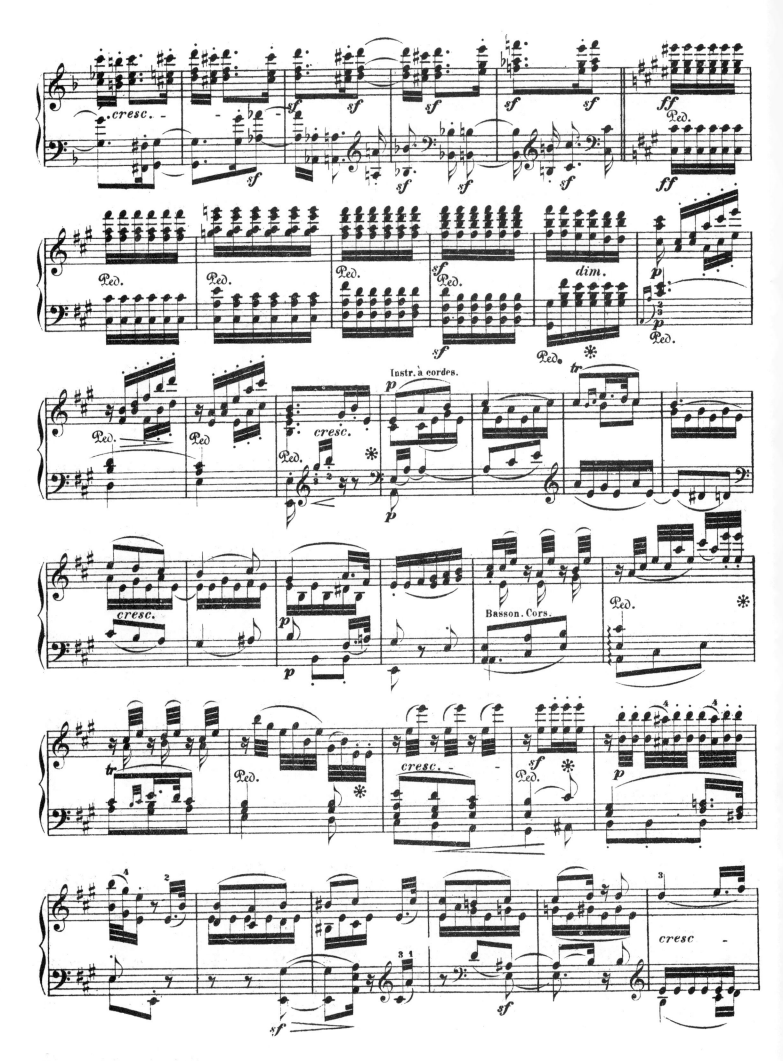

Symphony No. 3
in E-flat Major, Op. 55
("Eroica")

Scherzo.
Allegro vivace. (♩. = 116.)

Finale.
Allegro molto. (♩ = 76.)

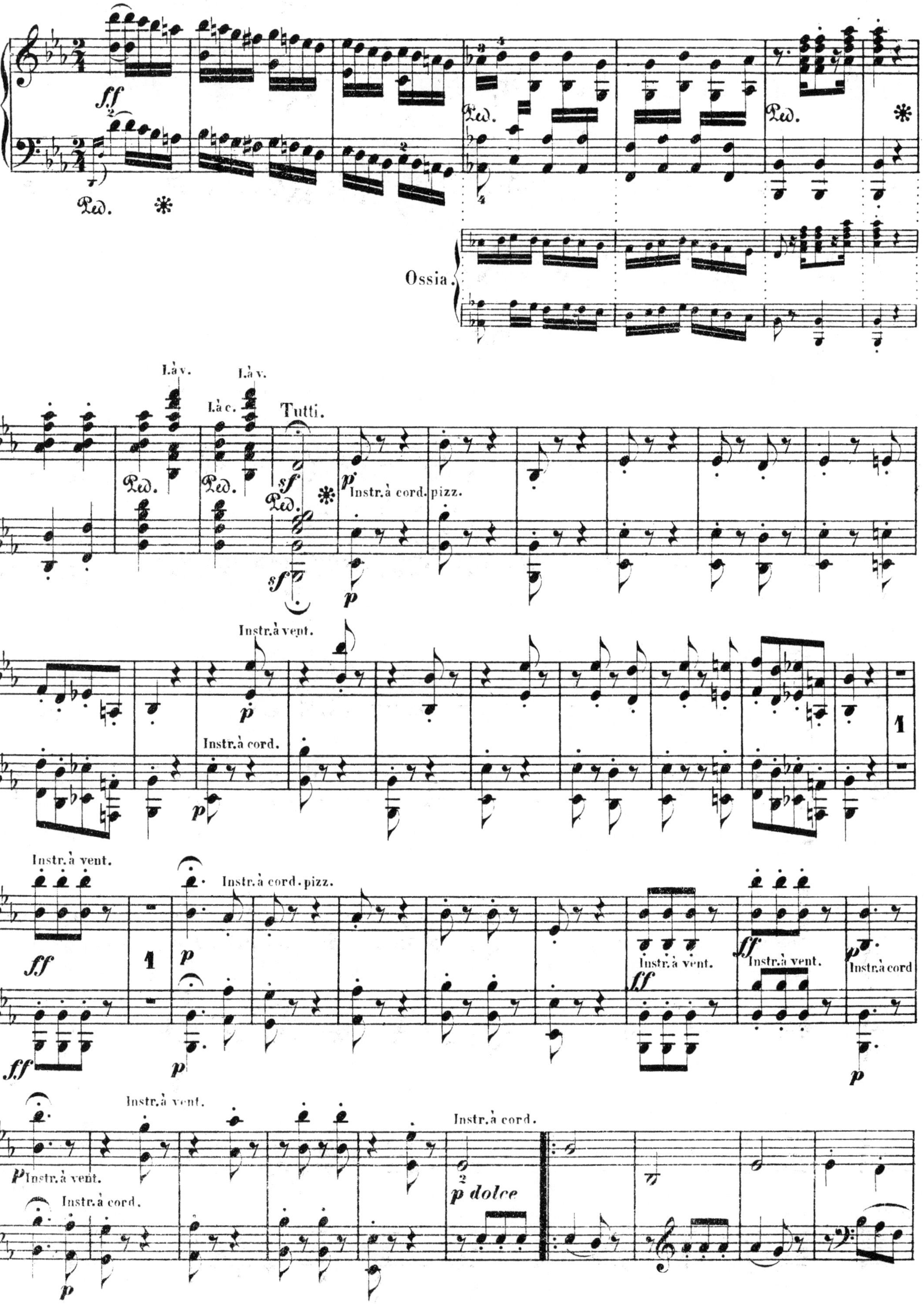

Symphony No. 4
in B-flat Major, Op. 60

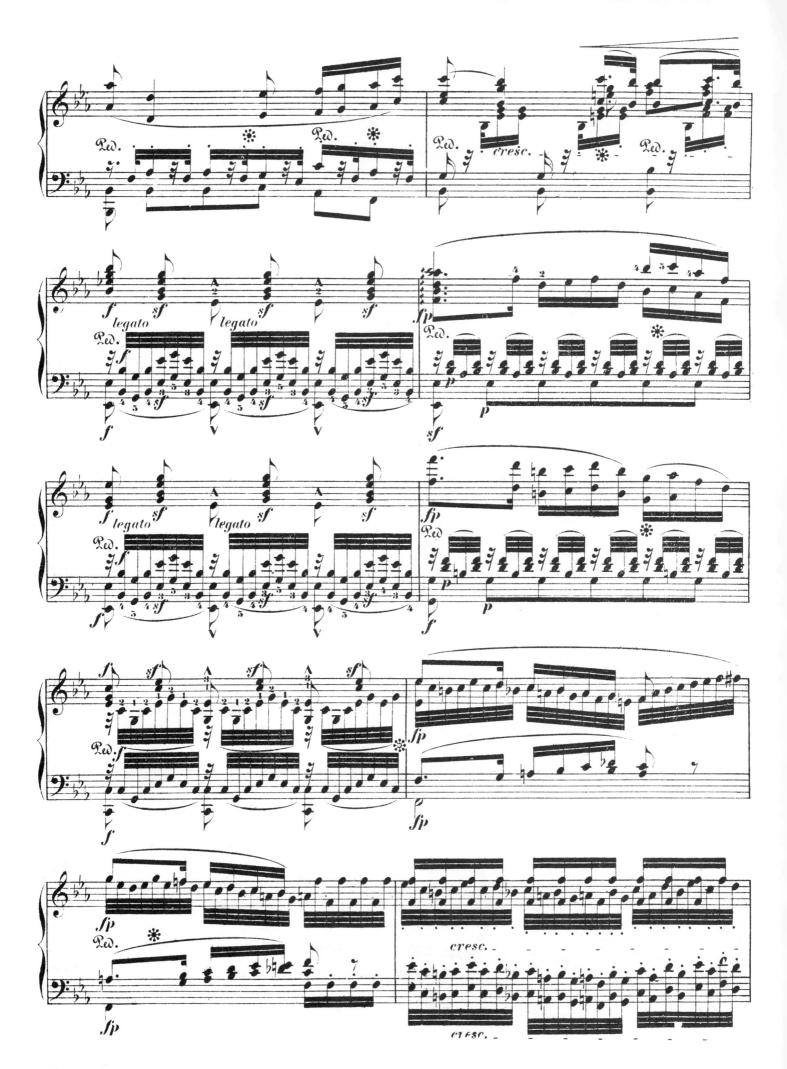

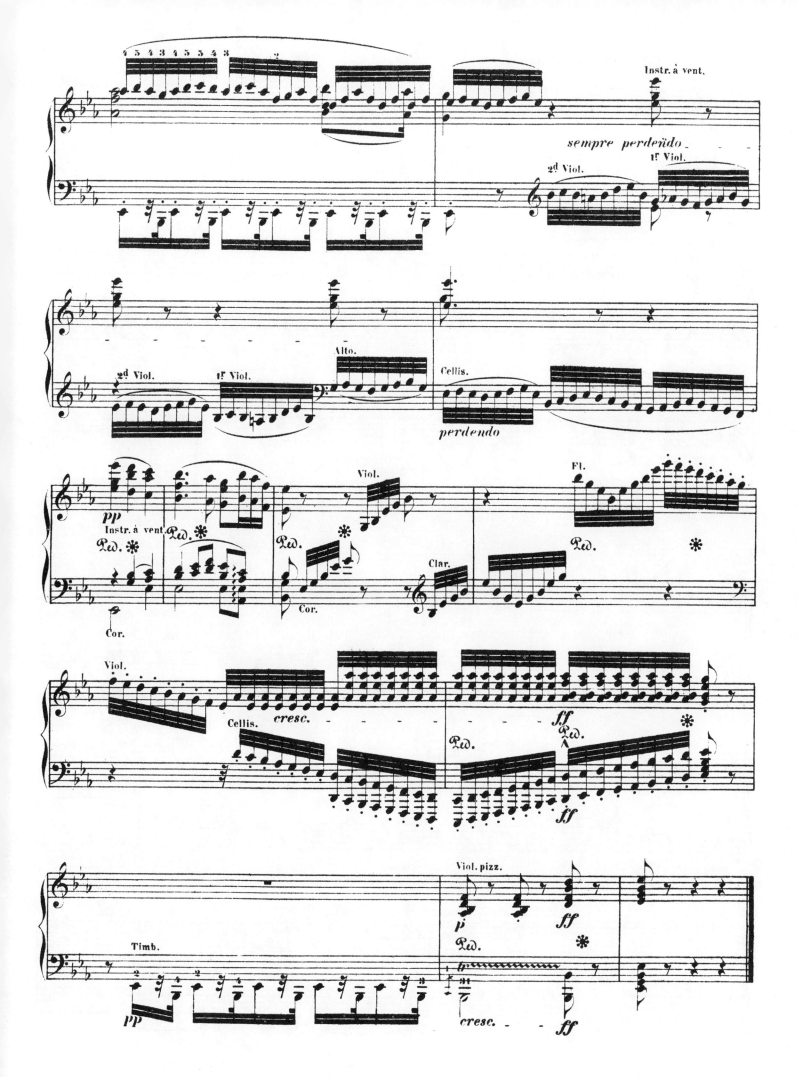

Allegro, ma non troppo.(♩ = 80.)

Symphony No. 5
in C Minor, Op. 67

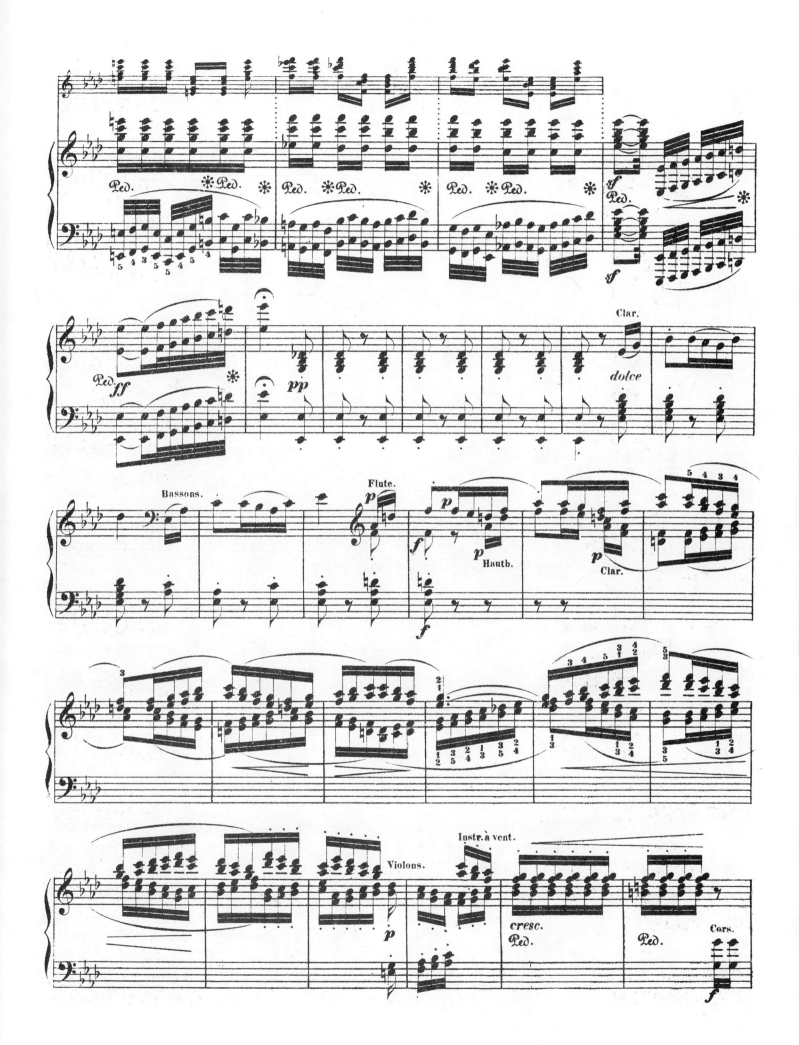

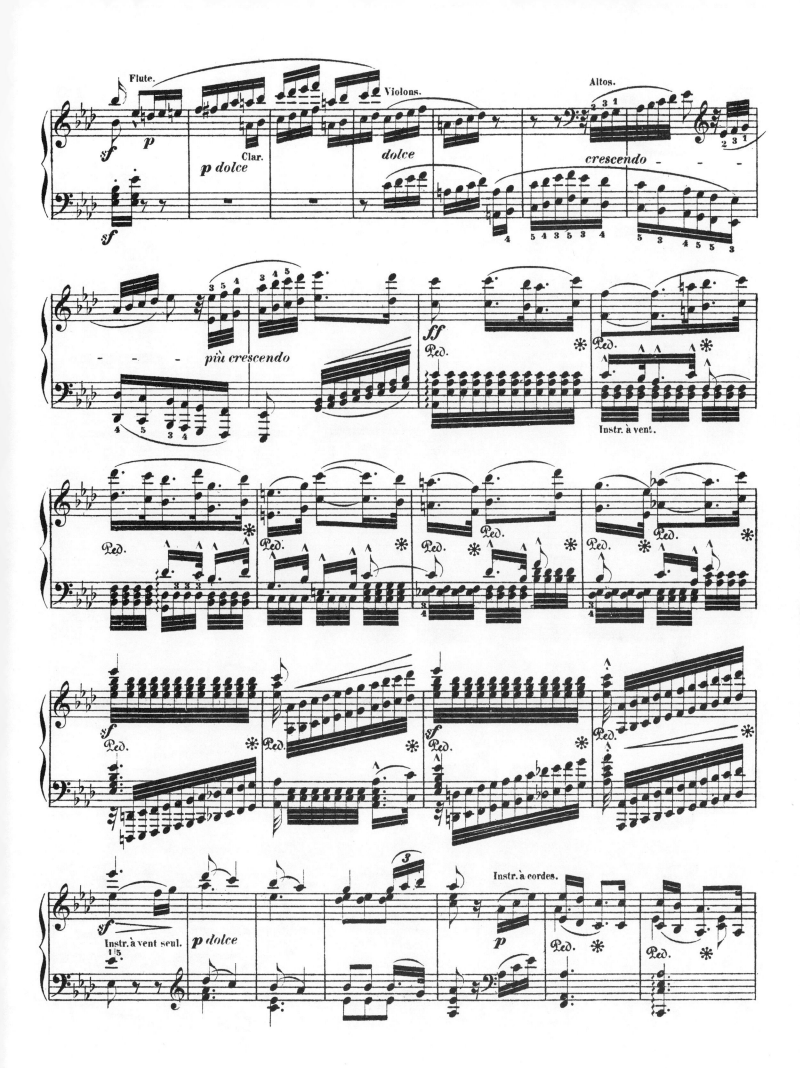